CHANGE YOUR THINK
COMPANION GUIDE

CHANGE YOUR THINK

COMPANION GUIDE

KRIS V. PLACHY, M.A.

ISBN-10   0983873615
ISBN-13   9780983873617
LCCN   2001012345

ALL RIGHTS RESERVED

Copyright © 2011 by Kris V. Plachy

All material in this book is the sole property of Kris V. Plachy. Reproduction or retransmission of this document, in whole or in part, in any manner, is prohibited without prior written permission from the copyright holder.

Hey Coach!

This is a guidebook designed to complement your work and learning from my book *CHANGE YOUR THINK*. I created this workbook so you would have more room and more opportunity to complete the exercises as you go through the book. There are also some additional exercises included to help you take a deeper dive into your thinking about leading, coaching, and managing. This is your place to reflect, ponder, and find the honest answers you need to develop yourself as a coaching leader. Make it messy. Enjoy the exploration of your thoughts! I think you'll find that you're even MORE amazing than you thought you were! Once you have gone through the process of changing how you think about your work, your team, your role as a manager, etc., you will have the tools you need for a lifetime.

You may find the companion **CHANGE YOUR THINK – JOURNAL** will be handy to keep with you during the day. It will help you process daily thoughts that occur in your work and with your team.

The goal of this work is to help YOU be stronger, more self-aware, and ultimately more successful as a manager, leader, and coach! Good luck and tell me your stories. I want to hear them!

All my best,

Kris

kris@krisplachy.com

CHANGE YOUR THINK Companion Guidebook

Let's get started!

In this section you're going to talk about yourself as a manager. Tell it all. The good, the bad, the great, and the stuff you hope no one ever really knows about you.

What makes you fabulous at what you do?

_____

_____

_____

_____

_____

_____

_____

_____

_____

If I asked other people about you as a manager-coach, what great things would they say about you?

_____
_____
_____
_____
_____
_____
_____
_____
_____
_____

Why do you think you are great at those things? What evidence do you have that reinforces your thoughts? How have you demonstrated your greatness?

_____
_____
_____
_____

_____
_____
_____
_____
_____
_____
_____
_____
_____

What thoughts do you believe about yourself that reinforce your greatness? Write those thoughts here:

(EXAMPLE: I am great in my role as a manager because I am honest with my team.)

- _____
- _____
- _____
- _____
- _____
- _____
- _____
- _____

Could you write down 10 thoughts? Why or why not? ("I can't think of 10" doesn't cut it).

_____

_____

_____

_____

_____

Now, let's talk about what gets in the way. What do you think you could do better and why? When you aren't good as a manager-coach, what are the reasons? What do you wish you could change about yourself as a manager-coach?

_____

_____

_____

_____

_____

_____

_____

_____

_____

If I asked, what would others say you could be better at as a manager or coach? What do you think other people wish you did more or less of? Why?

_____

_____

_____

_____

_____

_____

_____

_____

_____

When you believe you aren't effective as a manager-coach, what thoughts do you believe about yourself? Write those down here:

Example: I don't like to hold people accountable.

- _____

- _____

- _____

- _____

- _____

Lastly, what's the one thing you wish you could change about being a manager? This is the thing that bugs you, keeps you up at night. Makes you sometimes wonder why you signed up for the whole managing-others gig.

The one thing I wish I could change is:
_____

_____

*** We're going to come back to this work a little later in the guidebook.***

What is *CHANGE YOUR THINK?*: Chapter 2

What are your current coaching and managing challenges?

1. _____
2. _____
3. _____
4. _____
5. _____

Talk about it. What is the story behind each challenge?

1. _____

_____

_____

_____

_____

_____

_____

_____

2.

3.

4.

5.

Now, take a look at the story you've written for each challenge. What are the facts? What is provable (not just common knowledge or stuff you've gotten everyone to agree with you on)? ☺

Challenge #1

- _____
- _____
- _____
- _____

Challenge #2

- _____
- _____
- _____
- _____

Challenge #3

- _____
- _____
- _____
- _____

Challenge #4

- _____
- _____
- _____
- _____

Challenge #5

- _____
- _____
- _____
- _____

Okay, now let's see what thoughts you have *about* the facts.

Challenge #1

- _____
- _____
- _____
- _____

Challenge #2

- _____
- _____
- _____
- _____

Challenge #3

- _____
- _____
- _____
- _____

Challenge #4

- _____
- _____
- _____
- _____

Challenge #5

- _____

- _____

- _____

- _____

And these *thoughts* lead to *feelings*. What feeling comes up when you believe the thoughts you wrote above?

Thought: _____

    Feeling: _____

Thought: _____

    Feeling: _____

Thought: _____

    Feeling: _____

Thought: _____

    Feeling: _____

Thought: _____

    Feeling: _____

Thought: _____

    Feeling: _____

Thought: _____

    Feeling: _____

Thought: _____

    Feeling: _____

And when you *feel* these feelings how are you likely to *act?*

Thought: _____

    Feeling: _____

    Action: _____

Thought: _____

    Feeling: _____

    Action: _____

Thought: _____

    Feeling: _____

    Action: _____

Thought: _____

    Feeling: _____

    Action: _____

Thought: _____

    Feeling: _____

    Action: _____

Thought: _____

    Feeling: _____

    Action: _____

Thought: _____

    Feeling: _____

    Action: _____

Thought: _____

    Feeling: _____

    Action: _____

Thought: _____

    Feeling: _____

    Action: _____

Thought: _____

    Feeling: _____

    Action: _____

SELF-COACHING MODEL

CIRCUMSTANCE: a provable fact

⬇

THOUGHT: a sentence in your mind

⬇

FEELING: emotions

⬇

ACTION: behaviors

⬇

RESULT: the outcome of YOUR behavior

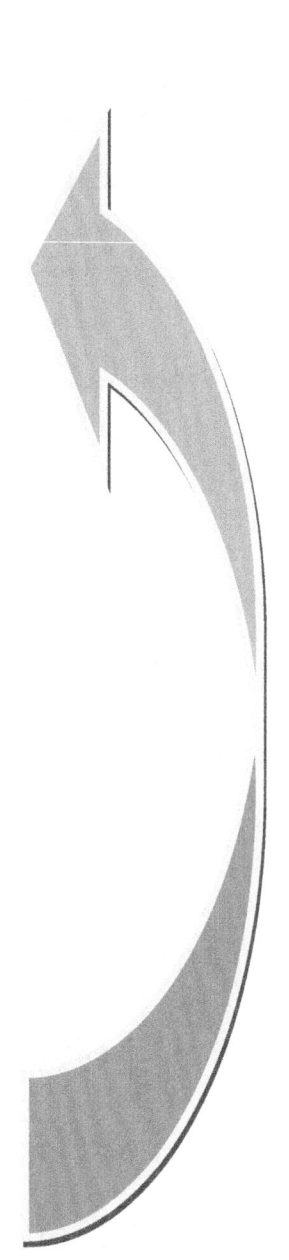

The result will always prove the originating thought true.

So let's think about some of the employees you wrote about in the Managing/Coaching Challenges exercise. How does what you believe about your employee(s) affect how you coach them?

EXAMPLE: My thought/belief that Lori is not engaged in her job affects my coaching because I spend less time with her, I don't give her big projects or assignments, and I have already started to think about who will replace her. I'm not helping create an environment that would engage her.

How does your thought/belief _____ about (employee)

_____ affect the way you coach?

_____

_____

_____

_____

How does your thought/belief _____ about (employee)

_____ affect the way you coach?

_____

_____

_____

_____

How does your thought/belief _____ about (employee)

_____ affect the way you coach?

_____

_____

_____

_____

Notice Yourself: FEEEEELINGS

Let's take a moment and play with your level of self-awareness.
Write down some feeeeeling words next to the following. Go with your first reaction.

When I'm with my boss, I feel

_____

List your employees and the feeling word that you attribute to each

_____

_____

_____

_____

When I don't meet a goal, I feel

_____

When I walked in the door at work today, I felt

_____

When I walked in the door at home today, I felt

_____

What's the one thing you enjoy most about being a manager?

_____

When you do this, how do you feel?

_____

What's the one thing you enjoy least about being a manager?

_____

When you do this how do you feel?

_____

The last time I felt happy,

    I felt _____ in my body.

The last time I was angry,

    I felt _____ in my body.

The last time I was scared,

    I felt _____ in my body.

Now let's explore the thoughts you have around the questions in the previous exercise. For each statement, write one thought that comes up (not a feeling).

When I'm with my boss, I think

_____

List your employees and the write one thought that you think about each.

_____
_____
_____
_____
_____
_____

When I succeed in my work, I believe

_____

When I don't meet a goal, I believe

_____

When I walked in the door at work today, I thought

_____

When I walked in the door at home today, I thought

_____

What's the one thing you enjoy most about being a manager?

_____

What's the one thing you enjoy least about being a manager?

_____

Since we're applying this learning to you as a manager, take a day at work and do the following exercise. Do it for the entire day. See what you find out.

Write down all of the people you interact with and experiences you had during the course of the day. Label each person and/or experience with a feeling word (happy, sad, worried, nauseous, etc.).

_____

_____

_____

_____

_____

_____

_____

_____

_____

Now, take each person/experience and the feeling state, and see if you can come up with a thought you had while dealing with that person or while you were in the experience (He talks too much, this meeting is boring, etc.).

_____

_____

_____

_____

_____

_____

_____

_____

_____

Based on what you thought and felt, how did you act? What were your results? Let's look at each component and place it in the model:

C: _____

T: _____

F: _____

A: _____

R: _____

C: _____

T: _____

F: _____

A: _____

R: _____

C: _____

T: _____

F: _____

A: _____

R: _____

C: _____

T: _____

F: _____

A: _____

R: _____

C: _____

T: _____

F: _____

A: _____

R: _____

The Coach & Accountability: Chapter 3

What is your belief about people who don't perform in their jobs?

_____

What is your belief about accountability as a manager?

_____

_____

Why (rephrase the thought above)?

_____

_____

Why (rephrase the thought above)?

_____

_____

Why (rephrase the thought above)?

_____

_____

Why (rephrase the thought above)?

_____

_____

How does your belief about accountability impact your ability to coach or manage others who aren't performing?

_____

_____

What potential roadblocks to coaching and managing performance may present themselves based on your beliefs about accountability?

_____

_____

When employees don't perform in their roles, I think:

_____

_____

When I think this, I feel:

_____

_____

When I feel this way, I act:

_____

_____

When I act this way, the results I get are:

_____

_____

Think of an employee that is currently not meeting performance expectations (as you define them). Answer the following:

What do you make their poor performance mean?

_____
_____

When you believe this thought, how do you feel?

_____
_____

When you feel this way, how do you act towards your employee?

_____
_____

When you act this way towards your employee what results do you get?

_____
_____

Let's do this for another employee:

What do you make their poor performance mean?

_____
_____

When you believe this thought, how do you feel?

_____
_____

When you feel this way, how do you act towards your employee?

_____

_____

When you act this way towards your employee, what results do you get?

_____

_____

One more....

What do you make their poor performance mean?

_____

_____

When you believe this thought, how do you feel?

_____

_____

When you feel this way, how do you act towards your employee?

_____

_____

When you act this way towards your employee, what results do you get?

_____

_____

Reworking Your Thoughts:

Using the thoughts you identified previously, let's see if we can change them up to improve your results. We'll start by identifying a new feeling we want to feel when we are coaching and managing our employee.

Challenge #1

Previous **Thought**:
_____

Previous **Feeling**: _____

How do you *want* feel when you are coaching and managing this employee?

New Feeling: _____

What do you have to believe about yourself or this employee to feel this feeling?

New Thought:
_____

Do the model:

C: _____

T: _____

F: _____

A: _____

R: _____

Challenge #2

Previous **Thought**:
_____

Previous **Feeling**:_____

How do you *want* feel when you are coaching and managing this employee?

New Feeling: _____

What do you have to believe about yourself or this employee to feel this feeling?

New Thought:

_____

Do the model:

C: _____

T: _____

F: _____

A: _____

R: _____

Challenge #3

Previous **Thought**:

_____

Previous **Feeling**:_____

How do you *want* feel when you are coaching and managing this employee?

New Feeling: _____

What do you have to believe about yourself or this employee to feel this feeling?

New Thought:

_____

Do the model:

C: _____

T: _____

F: _____

A: _____

R: _____

Challenge #4

Previous **Thought**:
_____

Previous **Feeling**: _____

How do you *want* feel when you are coaching and managing this employee?

New Feeling: _____

What do you have to believe about yourself or this employee to feel this feeling?

New Thought:
_____

Do the model:

C: _____

T: _____

F: _____

A: _____

R: _____

Challenge #5

Previous **Thought**:
_____

Previous **Feeling**:_____

How do you *want* feel when you are coaching and managing this employee?

New Feeling: _____

What do you have to believe about yourself or this employee to feel this feeling?

New Thought:
_____

Do the model:

C: _____

T: _____

F: _____

A: _____

R: _____

How will my coaching change once I've changed my thought about my employee(s)?
#1:

_____

_____

#2

_____

_____

#3

_____

_____

#4

_____

_____

#5

_____

_____

Remember what you wrote for the 'what keeps you up at night' question (on page 7). Time to look at that one:

The one thing I wish I could change is:

_____

_____

Why do you want to make this change?

_____

_____

What can you notice about your thoughts? What is the primary thought?

_____

_____

Let's do the Model:

C: _____

T: _____

F: _____

A: _____

R: _____

Rework it!

C: _____

T: _____

F: _____

A: _____

R: _____

Team Think & the Coach: Chapter 4

What common thoughts exist in your organization?

_____

_____

_____

_____

How do the thoughts impact your organization? Do the model.

C: _____

T: _____

F: _____

A: _____

R: _____

C: _____

T: _____

F: _____

A: _____

R: _____

C: _____

T: _____

F: _____

A: _____

R: _____

C: _____

T: _____

F: _____

A: _____

R: _____

How might these thoughts be reworked?

C: _____

T: _____

F: _____

A: _____

R: _____

C: _____

T: _____

F: _____

A: _____

R: _____

C: _____

T: _____

F: _____

A: _____

R: _____

C: _____

T: _____

F: _____

A: _____

R: _____

C: _____

T: _____

F: _____

A: _____

R: _____

Now let's talk about group thoughts that exist on your team. List them here:

_____
_____
_____
_____
_____
_____

How do the thoughts impact your team? Do the model.

C: _____

T: _____

F: _____

A: _____

R: _____

C: _____

T: _____

F: _____

A: _____

R: _____

C: _____

T: _____

F: _____

A: _____

R: _____

C: _____

T: _____

F: _____

A: _____

R: _____

How might these thoughts be reworked?

C: _____

T: _____

F: _____

A: _____

R: _____

C: _____

T: _____

F: _____

A: _____

R: _____

C: _____

T: _____

F: _____

A: _____

R: _____

C: _____

T: _____

F: _____

A: _____

R: _____

C: _____

T: _____

F: _____

A: _____

R: _____

How can you support your team to find new thoughts?

_____

_____

_____

_____

_____

Primary Question:

What questions do you ask yourself on a regular basis?
_____
_____
_____
_____

The *answers* to the questions you ask are thoughts that you believe.

For example: Why can't I lead a high performing team?
    Because I'm not a good leader.
    People don't respect me.
    My boss doesn't let me hire the right people.

What thoughts are derived from the questions you ask yourself?
_____
_____
_____
_____
_____
_____

Put those thoughts in the model:

C: _____

T: _____

F: _____

A: _____

R: _____

C: _____

T: _____

F: _____

A: _____

R: _____

C: _____

T: _____

F: _____

A: _____

R: _____

C: _____

T: _____

F: _____

A: _____

R: _____

The icky questions we are ask ourselves drive ineffective thoughts, which lead to poor results. When we *consciously* create a Primary Question we can intentionally create thoughts that support it.

For example: **How will I create a high performing team today?**
*I will engage with each team member.
I know the steps to take to reinforce excellent work.
I am the model of what I want my team to be*

.
What Primary Question can you create today?

_____

_____

What thoughts support this question?

_____

_____

_____

_____

_____

Put these thoughts in the Model:

C: _____

T: _____

F: _____

A: _____

R: _____

C: _____

T: _____

F: _____

A: _____

R: _____

C: _____

T: _____

F: _____

A: _____

R: _____

C: _____

T: _____

F: _____

A: _____

R: _____

C: _____

T: _____

F: _____

A: _____

R: _____

Identify one primary question that you really like and focus on that question for the next 30 days. See what happens. Experiment with how your life, work, etc. changes, just by reframing your daily experience with a new question.

_____

_____

Leadership Purpose: Chapter 5

Influences on who I am as a leader:

People:
_____
_____
_____
_____
_____

What impact has each of these people had on me as a leader?

Person_____

Impact_____

Person_____

Impact_____

Person_____

Impact_____

Person_____

Impact_____

Person_____

Impact_____

Leadership Purpose: Chapter 5

Places:

_____

_____

_____

_____

_____

What impact has each of these places had on me as a leader?

Place_____

Impact_____

Place_____

Impact_____

Place_____

Impact_____

Place_____

Impact_____

Place_____

Impact_____

Experiences:

_____

_____

_____

_____

_____

What impact has each of these experiences had on me as a leader?

Experience_____

Impact_____

Experience_____

Impact_____

Experience_____

Impact_____

Experience_____

Impact_____

Experience_____

Impact_____

What is most important to me as a leader?
_____
_____

What do I want people to remember about me?
_____
_____

What is my legacy?
_____
_____

What am I most passionate about?
_____
_____

What makes me unique?
_____
_____

What is your Leadership Purpose? (Remember keep it to a bumper sticker!)
_____
_____

How will knowing this purpose impact my coaching?
_____
_____

How will knowing this purpose impact my decisions?
_____
_____

Coaching Others With *Change Your Think*: Chapter 6

Why do you 'fix' employees? (Remember, this is a thought)
_____
_____

When you believe this, how do you feel?
_____

When you feel this way, how do you act?
_____

When you act this way, what results do you get?
_____

What is something else you can believe that will change your results?
_____
_____

When you believe this, how do you feel?
_____

When you feel this way, how might you act?
_____

When you act this way, what results might you get?
_____

Noticing your employees' thoughts:

Take the next several days and write down the thoughts you hear from your employees. Don't do anything about it. Just notice and write them down here:

_____

_____

_____

_____

_____

_____

_____

_____

_____

_____

_____

_____

_____

_____

_____

_____

List all of your employees and indicate a thought that they express on a regular basis:

Employee	Thought

Using the Self-Coaching Worksheets, go through each thought with each employee.

For example:

"John, I've heard you say that you don't think the goals we have for the team are reasonable. Is that true?" How do you feel when you believe this thought? And when you feel that way, how do you act? And when you act _____, what kind of results are you getting?

This works best when *they* see that their own thinking is driving their results. You can then help them rework their thought to achieve a better result.

SELF-COACHING WORKSHEET

Circumstance: (a provable fact or something that happened in the past)

_____

_____

When this happened, what did you make it mean?

Thought: (a sentence in your mind)

_____

_____

When you believe this thought, how do you feel?

Feeling: (one word)

_____

When you feel this way, how do you act?

Action: (one word)

_____

When you act this way, what results do you get?

Result:

_____

_____

SELF-COACHING WORKSHEET

Circumstance: (a provable fact or something that happened in the past)

_____

_____

When this happened, what did you make it mean?

Thought: (a sentence in your mind)

_____

_____

When you believe this thought, how do you feel?

Feeling: (one word)

_____

When you feel this way, how do you act?

Action: (one word)

_____

When you act this way, what results do you get?

Result:

_____

_____

SELF-COACHING WORKSHEET

Circumstance: (a provable fact or something that happened in the past)

_____

_____

When this happened, what did you make it mean?

Thought: (a sentence in your mind)

_____

_____

When you believe this thought, how do you feel?

Feeling: (one word)

_____

When you feel this way, how do you act?

Action: (one word)

_____

When you act this way, what results do you get?

Result:

_____

_____

SELF-COACHING WORKSHEET

Circumstance: (a provable fact or something that happened in the past)

_____

_____

When this happened, what did you make it mean?

Thought: (a sentence in your mind)

_____

_____

When you believe this thought, how do you feel?

Feeling: (one word)

_____

When you feel this way, how do you act?

Action: (one word)

_____

When you act this way, what results do you get?

Result:

_____

_____

SELF-COACHING WORKSHEET

Circumstance: (a provable fact or something that happened in the past)

_____

_____

When this happened, what did you make it mean?

Thought: (a sentence in your mind)

_____

_____

When you believe this thought, how do you feel?

Feeling: (one word)

_____

When you feel this way, how do you act?

Action: (one word)

_____

When you act this way, what results do you get?

Result:

_____

_____

SELF-COACHING WORKSHEET

Circumstance: (a provable fact or something that happened in the past)

_____

_____

When this happened, what did you make it mean?

Thought: (a sentence in your mind)

_____

_____

When you believe this thought, how do you feel?

Feeling: (one word)

_____

When you feel this way, how do you act?

Action: (one word)

_____

When you act this way, what results do you get?

Result:

_____

_____

SELF-COACHING WORKSHEET

Circumstance: (a provable fact or something that happened in the past)

_____

_____

When this happened, what did you make it mean?

Thought: (a sentence in your mind)

_____

_____

When you believe this thought, how do you feel?

Feeling: (one word)

_____

When you feel this way, how do you act?

Action: (one word)

_____

When you act this way, what results do you get?

Result:

_____

_____

SELF-COACHING WORKSHEET

Circumstance: (a provable fact or something that happened in the past)

_____

_____

When this happened, what did you make it mean?

Thought: (a sentence in your mind)

_____

_____

When you believe this thought, how do you feel?

Feeling: (one word)

_____

When you feel this way, how do you act?

Action: (one word)

_____

When you act this way, what results do you get?

Result:

_____

_____

SELF-COACHING WORKSHEET

Circumstance: (a provable fact or something that happened in the past)

_____

_____

When this happened, what did you make it mean?

Thought: (a sentence in your mind)

_____

_____

When you believe this thought, how do you feel?

Feeling: (one word)

_____

When you feel this way, how do you act?

Action: (one word)

_____

When you act this way, what results do you get?

Result:

_____

_____

SELF-COACHING WORKSHEET

Circumstance: (a provable fact or something that happened in the past)

_____

_____

When this happened, what did you make it mean?

Thought: (a sentence in your mind)

_____

_____

When you believe this thought, how do you feel?

Feeling: (one word)

_____

When you feel this way, how do you act?

Action: (one word)

_____

When you act this way, what results do you get?

Result:

_____

_____

SELF-COACHING WORKSHEET

Circumstance: (a provable fact or something that happened in the past)

_____

_____

When this happened, what did you make it mean?

Thought: (a sentence in your mind)

_____

_____

When you believe this thought, how do you feel?

Feeling: (one word)

_____

When you feel this way, how do you act?

Action: (one word)

_____

When you act this way, what results do you get?

Result:

_____

_____

SELF-COACHING WORKSHEET

Circumstance: (a provable fact or something that happened in the past)

_____

_____

When this happened, what did you make it mean?

Thought: (a sentence in your mind)

_____

_____

When you believe this thought, how do you feel?

Feeling: (one word)

_____

When you feel this way, how do you act?

Action: (one word)

_____

When you act this way, what results do you get?

Result:

_____

_____

SELF-COACHING WORKSHEET

Circumstance: (a provable fact or something that happened in the past)

_____

_____

When this happened, what did you make it mean?

Thought: (a sentence in your mind)

_____

_____

When you believe this thought, how do you feel?

Feeling: (one word)

_____

When you feel this way, how do you act?

Action: (one word)

_____

When you act this way, what results do you get?

Result:

_____

_____

SELF-COACHING WORKSHEET

Circumstance: (a provable fact or something that happened in the past)

_____

_____

When this happened, what did you make it mean?

Thought: (a sentence in your mind)

_____

_____

When you believe this thought, how do you feel?

Feeling: (one word)

_____

When you feel this way, how do you act?

Action: (one word)

_____

When you act this way, what results do you get?

Result:

_____

_____

SELF-COACHING WORKSHEET

Circumstance: (a provable fact or something that happened in the past)

_____

_____

When this happened, what did you make it mean?

Thought: (a sentence in your mind)

_____

_____

When you believe this thought, how do you feel?

Feeling: (one word)

_____

When you feel this way, how do you act?

Action: (one word)

_____

When you act this way, what results do you get?

Result:

_____

_____

Made in the USA
Monee, IL
20 June 2023